Butterflies

Edited by Heather C. Hudak

Published by Weigl Publishers Inc.
350 5th Avenue, Suite 3304, PMB 6G
New York, NY 10118-0069
Website: www.weigl.com

Library of Congress Cataloging-in-Publication Data

Hudak, Heather C., 1975-
 Butterflies / Heather C. Hudak.
    p. cm. -- (World of wonder)
 Includes index.
 ISBN 978-1-59036-866-4 (hard cover : alk. paper) -- ISBN 978-1-59036-867-1 (soft cover : alk. paper)
 1. Butterflies--Juvenile literature. I. Title.
 QL544.2.H83 2009
 595.78'9--dc22

                                    2008023851

Printed in the United States of America
1 2 3 4 5 6 7 8 9 0 12 11 10 09 08

Editor: Heather C. Hudak
Design: Terry Paulhus

Weigl acknowledges Getty Images as its primary image supplier for this title.

CONTENTS

What is a Butterfly?

Have you ever seen a pretty insect with paper-thin wings fluttering over a flower? This may be a butterfly.

A butterfly is a type of insect. There are more than 24,000 types of butterfly in the world.

Butterflies do not have a backbone.

Back in Time

Could you imagine living on Earth when the dinosaurs roamed? Butterflies first lived on Earth about 65 to 135 million years ago!

Some scientists think that butterflies came from moths. This happened around the time the first flowers began to grow on Earth.

Butterfly Life Cycle

What if you had hundreds of brothers and sisters? A female butterfly lays 200 to 500 eggs at one time. Caterpillars, or larvae, hatch from the eggs five days later.

As the caterpillar grows, it sheds its skin. After shedding for the last time, it becomes a pupa. The pupa stays inside a hard shell called a **chrysalis**. There, it slowly changes into a butterfly.

Caterpillar

Becoming a pupa

Chrysalis

Adult butterfly

What does a Butterfly Look Like?

Why do our bodies look so different from butterflies? Butterflies have three main parts to their body. These are the head, thorax, and abdomen.

The thorax has muscles that make the six legs and four wings move. Two **antennae** and **compound eyes** are found on the head. A hard shell, or exoskeleton, acts as a protective covering.

Butterflies range in size from 1.8 inches to 12 inches (4.5 to 30 centimeters). This is as small as a pin or as big as a chocolate bar.

antenna

head

abdomen

thorax

11

Saving Themselves

What if you had fragile wings that could tear easily? You would need to protect yourself from **predators**, such as birds, spiders, and reptiles.

Butterflies have special markings that help them blend into the environment. This makes it difficult for predators to see them. Some butterflies have patterns on their wings that look like giant faces. This helps scare away predators.

Butterflies weigh as little as two rose petals.

Have Wings, Will Fly!

How does a butterfly move through the sky? A butterfly has four delicate wings. There are two in the front and two at the back. Butterflies can fly as fast as 30 miles (48 kilometers) per hour .

When a butterfly comes out from the pupa, its wings are crinkled, wet, and flat. The butterfly hangs upside-down and pumps blood into the wings to make them grow to their full size.

15

What's for Dinner?

Have you ever used a straw to suck water from a tall glass? Butterflies have a long tube in their mouth that acts like a straw. They use this tube to suck **nutrients** from flowers.

Butterflies gather around shallow waters to drink on warm sunny days. This is called puddling.

Butterflies taste with their feet. They have taste **sensors** on their feet like the ones people have on their tongues.

17

Home Sweet Home

Butterflies can be found just about every place on Earth! They live in forests, marshes, deserts, jungles, and grasslands. Butterflies make their homes in tree holes.

Butterflies need flowers and fruits to survive. They settle in places that have these food sources.

Insect Lore

There are many stories about butterflies around the world.

Some people believe that seeing a white butterfly will bring good luck for an entire year. Other people believe that three butterflies together are bad luck.

In Scotland, some people believe that red butterflies are witches.

Draw a Butterfly

Supplies
Colored construction paper, a pencil, scissors, glue, tape, crayons, paint or markers, a pipe cleaner

1. Trace your hand on a piece of construction paper. Repeat six times.
2. Cut out the tracings. These will be the butterfly's wings.
3. On a piece of construction paper, draw a long oval and a small circle at one end. This will be the butterfly's body.
4. Glue the handprint tracings to the body, three on each side. The fingers should point outwards.
5. Fold a pipe cleaner in half. Curl the ends. The folded pipe cleaner will be the butterfly's antennae.
6. Tape the bent part of the pipe cleaner to the back side of the butterfly's head.
7. Draw eyes on the butterfly's head. Decorate the wings using crayons or markers.
8. Now you have a colorful butterfly.

Find Out More

To find out more about butterflies, visit these websites.

The Butterfly Site
www.thebutterflysite.com

Children's Butterfly Site
http://bsi.montana.edu/
web/kidsbutterfly

EnchantedLearning.com
www.enchantedlearning.
com/subjects/butterflies/
anatomy/Wings.html

FEATURE SITE:
www.butterflyschool.
org/student/
butterfly.html

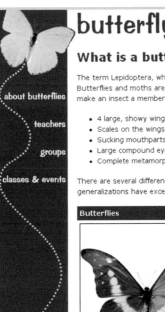

butterfly school

What is a butterfly?

about butterflies

teachers

groups

classes & events

The term Lepidoptera, which means "scaled wings" refers to butterflies and moths. Butterflies and moths are arthropods and insects. The special characteristics that make an insect a member of the Order Lepidoptera are:

- 4 large, showy wings
- Scales on the wings
- Sucking mouthparts (in those species which eat as adults)
- Large compound eyes in adults
- Complete metamorphosis

There are several differences between butterflies and moths, but all of these generalizations have exceptions! The main differences include:

Butterflies

Powered by Zoomify

Antennae:
Antennae are clubbed or hooked.

Moths

Powered by Zoomify

Antennae:
Antennae are either feathery, or pointed. There is no hook or club on the end.

Glossary

antennae: long, thin body parts that extend from an insect's head

chrysalis: a hard case covering the pupa of an insect

compound eyes: eyes that are made up of many small visual units

nutrients: substances needed in order for a living thing to grow

predators: animals that hunt other animals for food

sensors: dealing with one's senses

Index